What are TOYS Made of?

by Joanna Brundle

©2016
Book Life
King's Lynn
Norfolk PE30 4LS

ISBN: 978-1-910512-87-6

Written by:
Joanna Brundle

Designed by:
Drue Rintoul

A catalogue record for this book
is available from the British Library.

CONTENTS

You can find the **red** words in this book in the Glossary on page 24.

What is a TOY?

A toy is something which is made to be played with. Many different materials can be used to make toys.

All children enjoy playing with toys.

4

What is a
MATERIAL?

A material is what something is made of. Many toys are made using plastic, wood or metal.

Wood

Metal

Plastic

5

Toys made of
PLASTIC

Plastic is used to make toys because it is strong and light. It can be made into different shapes.

Building Bricks

Hula Hoop

Why do you think plastic is a good material for bath toys?

Many garden toys are made of plastic. This is because it is **waterproof** and it does not rot.

Swing & Slide

Sand Pit

Toys made of
WOOD

Wood is a natural material. Toys made of wood last a long time because wood is strong and does not break easily.

Dolls House

Rocking Horse

Old-fashioned toys, like spinning tops and toy soldiers, were made of wood.

Ask your grandparents if they played with wooden toys. Which one was their favourite?

Toy Soldier

Spinning Top

Toys made of METAL

Metal is used to make toys that need to be strong, like bicycles, scooters and pogo sticks.

Pushing the pedals harder makes you go faster.

Scooter

Bike

Have you got some toy cars? Which materials are they made of?

Models of cars, fire engines and trains can be made using metal.

11

Toys made of
GLASS AND CHINA

Marbles are made of coloured layers of glass. Some children collect marbles because they are very pretty.

Children playing marbles

Dolls used to be made of china. China breaks easily, so the children who played with them had to be gentle.

These dolls had real hair. Their faces were painted by hand.

13

Toys made of
PAPER AND CARDBOARD

Paper and cardboard are not as strong as plastic, wood or metal. Paper can be folded in special ways to make models.

These children have made paper aeroplanes.

Board games, like Ludo, are made of thick cardboard. Card games, like Snap, are made of thin card.

Children match the pictures on the board and the cards.

15

Toys made of
CLOTH AND FELT

Soft toys are made from different kinds of cloth, like cotton and velour.

The bear is furry and soft. What other words could you use to describe the bear?

16

Puppets

Felt and cloth can be used to make puppets.

Here are some birds and cars made of felt. What else could you make?

17

Toys made of
OTHER THINGS

Rubber is a natural material which is light and springy. It is great for making balls and bouncy toys.

18

You can find conkers on the ground in Autumn.

Conker

In some countries, children make their toys from things they find. Pebbles can be used for throwing and catching.

Toys made of RECYCLED MATERIALS

Materials that can be **recycled**, like cardboard boxes, are great for making toys.

A dragon and car made from cardboard boxes.

An old tyre makes a fun garden swing.

You can paint plastic drinks bottles to make skittles.

Can you think of a toy to make by recycling?

21

FUN FACTS

1 The yo-yo is one of the oldest toys in the world. Yo-yo tricks include "Atom Smasher" and "Walk the Dog".

2 The first toy advertised on television was Mr Potato Head.

3 The ingredients of Play Doh are kept a secret.

4 The first teddy bears were made of real fur, with eyes of glass or leather.

GLOSSARY

BOARD GAME
A game played by moving pieces round a board

FELT
A fabric made of wool fibres pressed together

NATURAL
Something made by nature not humans

OLD-FASHIONED
Not modern

RECYCLED
Something old that has been reused to make something new

RUBBER
A natural, stretchy material, made of tree sap or juice

VELOUR
A fabric with a very soft feel

WATERPROOF
Something that water cannot pass through

INDEX